a
life
speaks

Gloria House
2019 KRESGE EMINENT ARTIST

a
life
speaks

Edited by Nichole Christian
Art Direction by Patrick Barber
with contributions from
Larry Gabriel, Leslie Reese *and* ill Weaver/Invincible

THE KRESGE FOUNDATION

table

of

contents

foreword

Back in January 2019, hundreds of arts lovers gathered at Detroit's Masonic Temple for an evening of performances honoring our first decade of Kresge Eminent Artists.

We were reminded of the immense contributions to our community by sculptor Charles McGee; impresario David DiChiera; textile artist Ruth Adler Schnee; writers Bill Harris and Naomi Long Madgett; photographers Bill Rauhauser and Leni Sinclair; and musicians Marcus Belgrave, Patricia Terry-Ross and Wendell Harrison.

Closing that program, we proudly announced Dr. Gloria House as our 11th Eminent Artist, setting a high bar anew for our second decade.

Here we have a life of intimately interwoven activism, education and artistry.

Gloria House was on the forefront of a generation that changed America in the '60s. She joined the Free Speech Movement at University of California, Berkeley; she put her life on the line for civil rights in the Deep South; she helped give voice to the growing opposition to the Vietnam war.

Moving to Detroit in 1967 and making this area home, Gloria has called attention to police brutality, the prison-industrial complex, housing foreclosures, water shutoffs and other issues of fundamental equality. She has always engaged with the issues of the day.

Alongside activism and her work as an educator, a thread of poetry has run through her life. Mentored by the late Detroit Poet Laureate Dudley Randall, she has, in turn, become a mentor and example for young poets following his footsteps – and hers.

"We go on choosing life," Gloria wrote in her poem "Black Women's Affirmation."

Gloria, thank you for making choices that have affirmed and enriched our community.

RIP RAPSON
PRESIDENT AND CEO
THE KRESGE FOUNDATION

vi

artist's statement

gri·ot (/grē'ō, 'grēō/) *n.*

The griot is someone who celebrates the history, someone who does praise songs to the heroes, someone who officiates, someone who mediates conflicts, who brings understanding to the people.

    This is how I have been a poet, a poet very much embedded in the community and the words coming out of that rootedness, that engagement, fulfilling a lot of different roles that I hadn't seen as socially attributed to the role of poet in Euro-American society.

    In all of these roles, I've been honored to serve my community.

GLORIA HOUSE
2019

a
life
speaks

ever
forward

Gloria House's
Remarkable Journey
in Art and Activism

NICHOLE CHRISTIAN

In the final stanza of "Amiri Baraka: A Remembrance," poet Dr. Gloria House declares: "Your life testified."

In the poem, House pays homage to an iconic fellow poet and social justice activist. The words – just three – could also easily, and aptly, tell the story of her own immense five-decades-deep legacy as a poet, human and civil rights activist, organizer and educator.

Yet to know House – to spend any length of time in her presence – is to know a woman much too humble and still too forward-focused, even at age 78, to comfortably devote too much time to reflecting on the sum of her life. "It's too soon to know," she says in her quiet way. "I'm still here."

Indeed, House remains very much present with a near indefatigable presence in Detroit's literary, social justice, education and human rights circles. In 2017 she published *Medicine*, her fourth collection of poetry. Using her chosen African name, Aneb Kgositsile, House has written and published three other collections of poetry, each filled with passages from a life dedicated to standing against injustice. House was there at the start of the Free Speech Movement at the University of California, Berkeley. When she completed her studies and decided to head south to Selma, Alabama, to join the civil rights movement, her parents feared for her life. "We left the South," they told her, "We know what's down there."

Still, House kept moving, as she has decade after decade, lending

Gloria House reading from the first of her four poetry collections, *blood river*.

her voice, and vision, to the Black Arts Movement; the fight for voting rights, prisoner rights, and ongoing Detroit-based battles against police brutality, water shutoffs and illegal land use.

She is celebrated for poems of perseverance, praise and protest while leading a life in constant pursuit of justice and healing. "I'm not able to separate the artist's work," she says, "from the political work. It's where the poems come from."

Her unapologetic blending of the worlds of activism, art and education is at the center of House's selection as The Kresge Foundation's 2019 Eminent Artist. "Any single aspect of House's illustrious career as an activist, artist and educator could be considered a lifetime achievement," says Kresge President and CEO Rip Rapson. "Her accomplishments and influence in shaping culture over the course of several decades reflect a remarkable commitment to freedom of expression and the enrichment of the lives of others."

Gloria House is so *many* things, but first and foremost she's an artist. She makes us all see new possibilities through her actions. People around the country know her work and her words, and the way she's put her life on the frontline of important movements, all so that others could see the importance of their voices, and their own potential to change communities, maybe change the country.

—— **JUANITA MOORE**
Former President & CEO, The Charles H. Wright Museum
of African American History

House is the 11th artist to receive the prestigious honor. The Kresge Arts in Detroit office of the College for Creative Studies convened a panel of artists and arts professionals to make the selection. Kresge's award includes a $50,000 unrestricted prize. But for House the award has conferred something far more surprising and meaningful.

"I never thought I would win such an award because my work is so pointedly political. So, it's very special to me to know that other artists, cultural workers – people who know the terrain of the city – looked at the work I've done over the years and found beauty in it whether they agreed with the politics or not. It's wonderful to have such a public affirmation."

In Gloria House, there lives a quiet yet unrivaled model of artist-activist.

"There is no comma between artist and activist with Aneb," says Shea Howell, an Oakland University communications professor and longtime fellow organizer and friend. "Walk into any space where she is, and you immediately feel the enormous respect with which she's held, and that's for the whole of who she is: poet, writer, organizer, activist, rigorous scholar, mentor. She represents a lifetime from which people of all ages can learn."

> Moving to an ancestral beat,
> she be walkin' in rhythm
> with the people's music –
> they all be singin' their hearts out
> and she be travelin' right long with 'em[1]

Generations of poets, activists, and cultural scholars speak her name. They call her *Mama Aneb* with a booming reverence. And many trade stories, big and small, about the ways her poetry and lifetime of activism have helped shape their connection to and understanding of pivotal civil and human rights struggles. "Mama Aneb is a Detroit treasure," says Tawana "Honeycomb" Petty, author, poet and social justice organizer.

For the past half-century, she has dedicated herself to the cause of the need for the equal treatment of all. This well-deserved Kresge Eminent Artist Award will serve as a belated introduction to an even wider audience for this quiet, selfless but fierce warrior.

—— **BILL HARRIS**
Playwright, poet and 2011 Kresge Eminent Artist

"Mama Aneb has shown up for me with compassion as a human being and serves as a mentor for most of the identities I claim. This is a woman who has dedicated her life to the struggle for human rights and continues to do so today. She could retire and never lift another finger, and she will have done more than enough," Petty says.

Her consistent engagement is a particular source of inspiration for young socially conscious artists, observes Taylor Renee Aldridge, editor and co-founder of online journal Arts.Black. "Mama Aneb has not only shaped the network of poets and poetic platforms in the city, but she's nurtured and schooled many generations of organizing in Detroit. Mama Aneb is so deserving of this award," says Aldridge.

Adds Howell: "You can find people who speak the truth and you can find people who feel connected. But to have that sense of both legacy and future in a way that helps us all look at who we've been, and maybe who we'd like to become, is a tremendous gift when so much in Detroit, in the world, feels so uncertain."

Roots & Resistance

Only life to live.
Only a people to create
When she has come of age,
she carries in her the seed
of the people's new life.[2]

Gloria House was born Gloria Larry in Tampa, Florida, in 1941. But her roots and connection to the city had little chance to grow strong, to become home.

When House was 5, her mother remarried. He was a military man, Leroy Johnson, an airplane mechanic who rose quickly to the rank of chief master sergeant. Wherever the Air Force assigned her stepfather, House and her mother, Rubye, followed. "We ended up traveling everywhere." The family made stops in Salina, Kansas; Springfield, Massachusetts; Bermuda, England and finally, by the time House was nearing 11th grade, North Highlands, California, a suburb of Sacramento.

As her parents and baby sister, Patricia, 12 years younger, were finally settling in one place, House was mapping a new direction. By 16, she was a high school graduate on her way to study at nearby American River College, and then at the University of California,

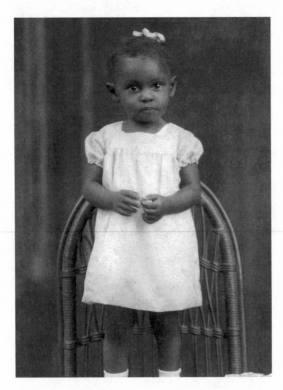

Gloria as a toddler.

Berkeley, thanks to a long-running scholarship endowment program made possible by the late blue-jeans co-inventor Levi Strauss. "I may not have been able to go if I hadn't gotten the scholarship, because my folks were not in a good place financially."

Yet buoyed by her parents' introduction to travel, the teenage House left home more curious than afraid. Even today she prizes her early exposure to travel, despite its impact on her childhood. "We only stayed in each place two or three years," she says. "So you couldn't really develop permanent community. It's one of the reasons why community circles, relationships, have been so important in my life."

And because hers was a family on the move, House has only a sparse collection of childhood mementos. "My folks didn't make childhood photos," she says. The typical treasured tales are few, too. "It was usually just the three of us. I didn't grow up with all my extended family around me."

The family member who loomed the largest in House's life was

Gloria looks at a cherished family photo of her maternal grandmother, Essie Ella Robinson.

PHOTO: PATRICK BARBER

her maternal grandmother, Essie Ella Robinson, a detail-oriented seamstress in Tampa known to keep one eye trained on the community's needs and the other on her family's. "She represented for me these values of justice and engagement with community in a personal way, as a part of who she was."

It was in her grandmother's front yard, in fact, that House had her very first brush with "resisting, standing up on my own."

"There was a tree in my grandmother's yard that I loved to swing on," she said. "It had really nimble, agile branches, so it made for really great swinging. My grandmother had told me many times, 'Please do not swing on the branches.'"

But, as House recalls, "Of course, there I was swinging." Eventually, her grandmother called her inside for an introduction to a distinctly Southern tool of punishment: the switch. "In the South, you didn't get spanked."

What happened next is now something of a family legend. "The story goes that I sort of stood there stoically for a while, and then after she'd been whipping my legs for a little bit, I said, 'I think that's enough now, Grandma. Don't you?'"

Though she died before seeing her brave grandchild blossom into a determined, history-making activist, House suspects her grandmother saw the seeds and was pleased. Her mother, now 99 years old, still recounts the tale. "My mom says my grandmother could barely hold in the howling. She had to go into another room and just crack up that this skinny little scrawny something was daring to tell her that's enough."

House's voice erupts into a rush of laughter at the memory – and the irony. "I guess I must have always had a sense of, what is fair here? Can I speak up for myself?"

Write, Little Girl, Write

Will words, in short,

keep us alive?

Let us call them ... [3]

She cannot pinpoint the age or the exact moment she began to write.

What Gloria House will tell you, with delight, is this: She was young, and it was love. "As a little girl, I was always writing. I would write little rhymes and poems. I can remember a play that I did in fourth grade, for Christmas. The sensitivity to words just came very early, and it's continued all the way."

She continues, "I still love that feeling when words are about to emerge. Sometimes the poem will just come, all of it, just one full complete thing. Sometimes."

Each poem, like each of her books, comes to life on its own terms at its own pace. "It's not that I sit down and say, OK, now I'm going to write this poem or this collection of poems," she explains. "It doesn't happen that way for me. Usually, there is a beat or a rhythm or a mood

Gloria reads during a Wayne State University poetry conference.

Gloria proudly shares a copy of her poetry collection *Rainrituals* with the late South African leader Winnie Mandela in Detroit.

that signals there's a poem coming. My job is to listen and let the words emerge."

It's a process that's guided House through the publication of four poetry collections: *blood river* (1983), *Rainrituals* (1989), *Shrines* (2013) and *Medicine* (2017). Each of the books exists in part because of a hunch acted upon by Detroit's first poet laureate and founder of the legendary Broadside Press, Dudley Randall. During a visit to her home, House recalls Randall inquiring whether she wrote poetry.

"You must write poetry," he insisted. At the time she was a Broadside Press volunteer. "Yes, Dudley," she recalls answering reluctantly, "I do."

The tattered manila folder House shared with Randall that day became her debut book, a collection that Randall himself laid out. He even invited House to design the cover art. "I think we forgot to include the art credit," House says with a wry smile.

Like Randall, she continues to be a guide for emerging poets in her current role as senior editor at Broadside Lotus Press and as the series editor for the Naomi Long Madgett Award, a celebrated competition

Gloria at age 20, upon graduating from the University of California, Berkeley in 1961.

for African American poets. (Madgett is Detroit's current poet laureate and the 2012 Kresge Eminent Artist.)

At Madgett's request, she revived the competition as part of Broadside Press's merger with Lotus, which Madgett founded. "To pick up where she left off has been a real honor and part of an important legacy," House says.

House writes the way she speaks, with passion, precision and sharp, unmistakable pride in her culture. "I don't want people to have to wonder what I'm trying to say," she explains. "A lot of poets celebrate difficulty, being complicated, playing with language. I'm trying to share a particular perspective by painting the picture that I see and hoping people can see but also that they can feel the love that infuses each word."

Yet as central as words have always been in House's life – she holds a master's degree in comparative literature from the University of California, Berkeley – only in recent years has she grown comfortable seeing "poet" beside her name.

"I didn't claim that for a very, very long time," she says. "Part of that had to do with the fact that in the United States and the Western world there are certain conventional ideas and images associated with poets. I knew I didn't fit into any of those boxes."

But after reading "some very serious scholarship" on the role of the griot in Western African culture, House finally found a way to see her great love of words in a broader cultural context. "The griot is someone who celebrates the history, someone who does praise songs to the heroes, someone who officiates, someone who mediates conflicts," she explains.

"This is what I've been doing. This is how I have been a poet, a poet very much embedded in the community, the words coming out of that rootedness, that engage, fulfilling a lot of different roles that I hadn't seen associated with poets in Euro-American society."

Today, House claims her creative identity with joy. "I now understand the multiplicity of roles that someone who works with language can fulfill," she explains. "I feel finally able to say, yes, I am a poet."

For Freedom's Sake

Can't sit still, no, I can't sit down.
Can't sit down, no, I can't sit down ... [4]

Gloria House is – on paper, at least – retired.

She's gone through the official motions twice, first from Wayne State University in 1998 where she taught for 27 years and again in 2014 from the University of Michigan–Dearborn, where she designed and directed the African and African American Studies Program.

The only measures by which House considers herself a retiree are her age, and the fact that she hasn't taken on another salaried position. "I don't think I will," she says.

Yet her work as an educator presses on. House co-founded the Detroit Independent Freedom Schools Movement on the model of her work in Lowndes County, Alabama, where she helped the Student Nonviolent Coordinating Committee (SNCC) launch voter registration drives and set up its Selma Freedom School. On Saturdays, she's present at the Charles H. Wright Museum of African American History for Freedom School, which offers free tutoring and enrichment to dozens of preteen children. "I'm not always in front of the classroom; sometimes it's getting the teacher to the classroom."

Fellow activists say the real poetry of Gloria House's life is evident in the artful ways she's used her longevity to organize community and to activate ideas.

"All of the separate parts of Gloria House are fascinating," says Malik Yakini, founder of the Detroit Black Community Food Security Network, D-Town Farm and the Detroit People's Food Co-op. "But when you look at them as a lived life, one that's still creating, it's really remarkable."

Yakini met House in the early 1980s. His admiration grew watching House lead the campaign to free Ahmad Rahman, a former Black Panther sentenced to life in prison for a murder he insisted he didn't commit. House met Rahman while teaching classes at the former Jackson State Prison through Wayne State University. House

Gloria protests for the release of Ahmad Rahman, a Black Panther whom she mentored. Following his release from prison, Rahman went on to become an award-winning professor at the University of Michigan–Dearborn.

PHOTO: LENI SINCLAIR, 2016 KRESGE EMINENT ARTIST.

volunteered for what was supposed to be an experimental teaching assignment. Three years later, it had turned into much more.

Rahman became one of her star students (and the first Michigan inmate to receive an undergraduate degree); his freedom became one of House's greatest drives for justice. In 1992, Rahman won a gubernatorial pardon after serving 22 years. With House's help, he went on to become a professor of African and African American Studies at the University of Michigan–Dearborn. "I'm proud of what we accomplished," she says. "He had so much to offer with his life."

Any attempt to separate House the artist from House the activist erases her most enduring gift, Yakini says. "She demonstrates a sense of wholeness that a lot of people fighting to make a better world often forget. It's possible to bring all of who you are to all that you do. She's been able to be this cutting-edge poet who has mastery of the language, but at the same time her poetry is informed by this very deep longing for freedom that's she's personally fought for."

Over the years, others have asked what keeps House engaged. The answer almost always comes back to the movement, to the bloodshed she witnessed, and the voices she helped cry out for justice. "The SNCC experience disciplined me for a lifetime of struggle. It's still true to me that one is never a retired civil rights worker."

Of course, House foresees the day when her steps start to slow and her presence becomes more select. "As I get older," she says, "and my energy starts to decline, I will probably do more writing and teaching and less picketing. But I don't feel I could ever just sit on the sidelines. I don't want to, not when there's so much work still to be done toward social justice. I wouldn't be happy sitting."

Sweet Home Detroit

We must sing our song again
and summon the will to stand
like those proud 19th Century African men and women in Detroit
who, in the face of relentless intimidation,
built churches and schools and mutual aid societies
and harbored those running to Canada for freedom[5]

Gloria House chose Detroit in winter: January of 1967 to be exact. "It's the first city I ever saw as home."

She was newly married to fellow activist and demographer Stuart House and fresh from the battlefield that was Lowndes County, Alabama. The Motor City, her husband's birthplace, seemed the perfect place to write a new chapter, to welcome the new life on the way, a son named Uri, her only child.

"When I first came to Detroit, it was just so beautiful, the homes, the neighborhoods. You could feel the historical legacy of this working-class city, in the music, in the brilliant workers who were creating new ideas and organizing for real change."

By July of '67, however, House watched her new hometown become an eerily familiar battleground sparked by a series of confrontations between police and citizens. "I didn't have a sense of any

Gloria in Lowndes County with SNCC working as a field secretary and voting rights organizer.
PHOTO: DOUG HARRIS

impending rebellion," she says referring to what would become one of the 1960s' most violent urban American rebellions. "But when it began I could see there was a definite political divide in the city. Black leadership could not speak to the people who were on the streets. The divide was very open."

But never once did the rebellion, or the tensions after, taint her view of Detroit. "Certainly, I wasn't frightened or turned off, having enough political orientation to watch and understand, well, this is about demanding greater rights, a better city."

Over time, House would join many of the calls for a more just Detroit. She was fired from a job at the *Detroit Free Press* as an editorial page copy editor for taking part in a demonstration against STRESS, the infamous Detroit Police unit that operated under an acronym for "Stop the Robberies, Enjoy Safe Streets."

House was offered a chance to return to work, a 3 p.m.-to-midnight shift, but she declined. Uri had just entered kindergarten, and she wanted to spend evenings with him. Furthermore, she was uninterested in muting her voice.

She found work at Wayne State University. She also found kinship and a community of mentors in gatherings with some of the city's leading political and social progressives, including Grace and Jimmy Boggs, and Martin and Jessie Glaberman. To House, both couples were towering influences for their respective work as labor and civil rights organizers, scholars and writers. "I had the benefit of so much brilliant new thought and activism often at the dinner table on Sundays when we'd gather."

Close friendships became even more valuable to House by 1974, when she and her husband divorced. Her mother assumed she'd finally return to California to raise Uri there. But Detroit was already "home," and well on its way to nurturing her politically and creatively just as the South had done in her youth.

Now, 52 years after her move, House looks out over Detroit from her riverfront apartment with a mix of love and heightened concern.

"To come to this point in the city's history," she says, "where so many jobs have been lost, so many people have lost homes to

TOP LEFT: Gloria's former press badge.

TOP RIGHT: Gloria reads a worn copy of Wayne State University's *South End* newspaper, featuring an article about her dismissal from the *Detroit Free Press*.

PHOTO: PATRICK BARBER

CLOCKWISE FROM LEFT:

The House family's first home in Detroit on Ewald Circle.

Gloria and her son Uri at her retirement from Wayne State University.

Gloria standing with young son Uri over her shoulder.

Gloria with her mother, Rubye M. Johnson (center), and her sister, Patricia E. Johnson (right).

Gloria celebrates Uri's graduation from Tuskegee University with his father, Stuart House.

DETROIT PRESS
POLICE and FIRE CARD
DEPARTMENTS
PASS (On all proper occasions and subject
to the rules of both departments.)
THROUGH ALL POLICE AND FIRE LINES
HOUSE, Gloria
Representing
THE DETROIT FREE PRESS

Board of Fire Commissioners, President
Police Commissioner

1971

Woman fired from Free Press for political

Gloria visits the grave of South African revolutionary leader Chris Hani. Gloria served as a visiting professor in the English Department of the University of Witswatersrand (WITS) from 1992 to 1995. Part of her work included creating and directing the WITS Partnership with Township High Schools.

foreclosures; have experienced unjust water shutoffs, eroding neighborhoods and schools still struggling, it's easy to become bitter."

But easy choices have never appealed to House. The willingness to engage troubling questions and unknowns in the midst of struggle, she says, is where one becomes most creative, most alive. "We don't have the power, we don't have the money," she says, "We do have the ability to become more conscious, to come together in ways that value community and allow us to ask, what do people need to live good lives? How can we sustain each other?"

It's a full-circle moment for House. Much like her elders did during the 1960s, she is looking to the ideas of the youth. "I'm hoping that young organizers and artists won't be discouraged by what looks like so much power benefitting so few; that they'll go on imagining, conceiving, dreaming of new ways to live in the city and make it just.

"A poet, an artist can be involved in creating answers, creating change. You can create a life of use," she says. "I certainly hope that's some of what I've done."

> Let the words slide into silence
> Let thought slip through the lace of days like
> light rays through parted curtains
> Let truth speak through my hands.[6]

Nichole Christian is a writer and veteran journalist. She is co-author of *Canvas Detroit*. Her writing also appears in *Portraits 9/11/01: The Collected "Portraits of Grief" from The New York Times*; the online arts journal, *Essay'd: A Detroit Anthology* and *Dear Dad: Reflections on Fatherhood*.

This essay features excerpts from the following poems written by 2019 Kresge Eminent Artist Gloria House:
1. "Seed of the People's New Life," published in *blood river*.
2. "Seed of the People's New Life," published in *blood river*.
3. "Incantation," published in *blood river*.
4. "Possession Dance," published in *Shrines*.
5. "We Will Stand," published in *Medicine: New and Selected Poems*
6. "I Want to Make Beautiful Things," published in *Medicine: New and Selected Poems*.

chasing justice

justice

From Berkeley to Bloody Lowndes

LARRY GABRIEL

To understand Gloria House as

an artist is to know her as a lifelong activist fighting for freedom and human rights. It was on a trip to France in 1961 that she first engaged political ideals. There she met African students who were fighting racism and colonialism around the world.

"That was a kind of awakening to myself as an African person belonging to a much bigger world than the United States," says House. "When I came back home, I was looking at everything from a different perspective and understood political struggles. I was ready to be engaged, looking for an opportunity to lend my energies to the civil rights movement."

In graduate school, House was a teaching assistant in the French department at the University of California, Berkeley during the 1964–65 Free Speech Movement, a massive, long-term protest aimed at lifting the ban on students' on-campus political activities – particularly around civil rights and anti-war issues. During the occupation of one of the school buildings, teaching assistants taught what were dubbed "freedom classes." It was the beginning of a style of activism-by-teaching that has permeated House's life.

"We won the right to continue organizing on campus," says House. "We won the right to unionize, the first teaching assistants in the country to form a union. It was an important struggle, and from there I ran into a group of San Francisco State University students who were going to Selma (Alabama) to set up a freedom school in the summer of '65. That's how I ended up going south."

That summer, House joined the efforts of the Student Nonviolent Coordinating Committee, popularly known as SNCC, in Alabama. SNNC had been formed to give young black organizers a voice in the civil rights movement. The organization served as the training ground of leaders such as Congressman John Lewis, the late NAACP Chairman Julian Bond, and Black Panther spokesmen H. Rap Brown and Stokley Carmichael (later known as Kwame Ture).

House taught basic reading skills, writing and composition, as well as a little French in the mornings. In the afternoons she worked with Carmichael, who became SNCC chairman, and others on voter registration, organizing an independent political party, and picket lines protesting discrimination. SNCC was financially sustained partly by donations from scores of Northerners who supported efforts

Sharecropper homes in Lowndes County, Alabama, where Gloria and other SNCC activists worked to register black voters in the 1960s.

Aneb has steel in her. Anyone a lot younger would have a hard time keeping up. She traverses local, national and international boundaries, creating sacred spaces as a poet, a fighter and a grassroots educator. She's made an art of elevating the individual and the group at the same time, and people feel the love she has for serving and for community.

—— **REV. SANDRA SIMMONS**
Educator, activist, co-founder of
Hush House Black Community Museum

like its voting rights campaign, which registered 2,500 black voters between 1965 and 1969.

During a picket in Fort Deposit, House was arrested along with 29 protestors. Five were soon released, but the others languished behind bars in Hayneville for six days before their release. Within walking distance of the jailhouse, a shotgun-wielding sheriff's special deputy fired on them. Jonathan Daniels, a white Episcopal seminarian, was shot dead. A white Episcopal priest, Father Richard Morrisroe, was gravely wounded.

"They forced us out of jail to a setup," House says. "They intended to kill the two white members of our group. ... Jonathan was only a few feet away from me when he was murdered. We thought we were all going to be shot down."

Despite the trauma, House continued her SNCC field work and shortly thereafter married fellow activist Stuart House. When she became pregnant they moved to Stuart's hometown, Detroit. "We thought we'd have the baby and go back to Alabama," she says, " but one thing led to another and here we are."

She taught French at Cass Tech High School, then worked briefly

LEFT: Gloria with former SNCC comrade and leader Stokely Carmichael (aka Kwame Ture) during a visit to Detroit in the late 1970s.

BELOW: Front page clipping from the *Detroit Free Press.*

ON GUARD FOR 168 YEARS

Detroit Free Press

METRO FINAL

THURSDAY
February 17, 2000

50 cents outside 6-county metropolitan area **35 cents**

WILLIAM ARCHIE/Detroit Free Press

Gloria House, 61, was one of the volunteers who survived her civil rights activism. She saw fellow workers Jonathan Daniels and Richard Morrisroe shot down in Hayneville, Ala. Daniels died.

Volunteer survived the shadow of death

But years later, justice denied in civil rights case

BY RUBY L. BAILEY
FREE PRESS STAFF WRITER

HAYNEVILLE, Ala. — The facts were never in dispute. Tom Lemuel Coleman shot and killed a seminary student with a 12-gauge shotgun, then shot a young priest in the back as the priest fled.

For Gloria House, the events of that day — Aug. 20, 1965 — are still vivid. House saw Coleman block a store entrance as a group of civil rights workers tried to enter. She saw the point-blank blast that lifted the seminary student into the air and robbed the

life from his body by the time he hit the ground.

And as House fell onto the dirt road to protect herself, she heard the second shot that nearly took another life.

What might have seemed like a

BLACK HISTORY MONTH

► Commentary: Reparation. **10A**
► Calendar of history events. **4B**

clear-cut case of murder and attempted murder wasn't clear cut then in Southern towns like Hayneville. Hayneville is in Lowndes County, where lynchings occurred into the 1960s. It had long ago earned its surname: Bloody.

Although Coleman went to trial, he wasn't convicted. House and others say there was no way he would have been, not then.

"That community was not about to turn on him," said House, a retired Wayne State University professor who moved to Detroit in 1967.

Please see RIGHTS, *Page 6A*

FATAL GUNSHOT IN 1965

Tom Coleman, left, stopped 26-year-old Jonathan Daniels, right, and other activists with a 12-gauge shotgun at the door of a Hayneville, Ala., store. Witnesses say Coleman shot Daniels at point-blank range.

In 1971 Gloria (right) interviewed Kathleen Cleaver for a story about the split in the Black Panther Party between members in Algeria and in the U.S. Kathleen was living in Algeria and on a tour of the U.S.

Also on the right is Frank Ditto, head of East Side Voice of Independent Detroit, a former community organization.

at the *Detroit Free Press* before landing at Wayne State University for 27 years teaching African American literature, American culture and research methods. After that, she spent 10 years developing the curriculum for African and African American Studies at the University of Michigan–Dearborn.

When she first arrived in Selma, dressed professionally and speaking in soft, cultivated tones, I wagered that she wouldn't be able to take more than a month of our rough-and-tumble existence. But she was a lot tougher than she looked. Bringing an international perspective, and a familiarity with political literature, Gloria played a major role in defining SNCC's nationalism, and globalism, particularly our opposition to the Vietnam War.

—— **MARTHA PRESCOD NORMAN NOONAN**
Civil rights activist, co-editor, *Hands on the Freedom Plow: Personal Accounts by Women in SNCC*

Teaching has been a major part of how House has endeavored to connect people to social change. She led curriculum design and served as both a volunteer teacher and board member for Aisha Shule, Timbuktu Academy and Nsoroma Institute, all African-centered schools in Detroit, and more recently the Detroit Independent Freedom Schools Movement, which offers weekend tutoring to middle school students at the Charles H. Wright Museum of African American History and other locations.

"There's an educational activism line that runs through her history and career," says Rev. Bill Wylie-Kellerman, progressive activist

Gloria at a 50th anniversary commemoration for SNCC in Raleigh, North Carolina, in 2010.

and retired former pastor of St. Peter's Episcopal Church in Detroit. "The nature of her commitment is to nonviolent struggle for freedom and is particularly rooted in the African diaspora. ... It's amazing how many people look to her as a sort of lodestar in the movement."

When Gloria House arrived in Detroit, she became active in local and worldwide freedom, civil rights, and peace and labor struggles. She soon met James and Grace Lee Boggs, political activists and philosophers with worldwide prominence and the inspiration for the Boggs Center to Nurture Community Leadership. The Boggs Center has helped to prepare a new generation of progressive activists facing crises. House has been part of that, currently co-editing its quarterly magazine *Riverwise*.

"Gloria was close to Grace," says Wylie-Kellerman, "going back to Poletown before they were the Boggs Center." The Poletown neighborhood on the Detroit–Hamtramck border was the site of a 1980s struggle that ultimately displaced more than 1,500 homeowners and businesses in favor of a new General Motors plant.

Dislocation and local rights continue to stir House's more recent activism. She works with Detroiters Resisting Emergency Management, a group that has helped to mobilize community awareness and resistance to a state law that allows the state to assume control of local governments in a financial crisis. Some cite the law, considered one of the broadest of its kind in the U.S., as a contributing factor to the the 2013 Detroit bankruptcy, the 2014 Flint Water Crisis, where citizens were unknowingly subjected to a tainted water supply, and repeated battles over the Detroit Public Schools system.

ABOVE: Gloria speaks at a 1998 public hearing on behalf of the Detroit Coalition Against Police Brutality and its demand that the Detroit City Council take action. House co-founded the DCAPB in 1996.

LEFT: Timbuktu Academy students throw a surprise going-away party for Gloria as she leaves her roles as principal and curriculum developer to head African and African American Studies at the University of Michigan–Dearborn.

In the case of Detroit's public schools, House and others focused on the children. "What was happening in schools? What deficits were children going to have? There were two or three generations of children who had not been educated well in Detroit schools. We decided that, rather than just sit and bemoan the situation, we would engage ordinary people, volunteers to set up in churches, et cetera, and invite children to come in for educational cultural activities."

The other group, We the People of Detroit, has taken on the water crisis in Flint from the practical standpoint of supplying fresh, clean water to people. In Detroit, the group has been a vocal opponent of water shutoffs, and has examined the causes of the policy. In 2016, We the People of Detroit published a booklet, *Mapping the Water Crisis: The Dismantling of African-American Neighborhoods in Detroit*. It shows the public health impacts of water shutoffs and the racial impacts of the regional water board's policies.

"We were able to do fantastic maps of the water situation, areas where people were being deprived, always African American areas," says House, who edited and helped to design the publication. Today, it's presented in university classrooms, another link between House's activism and education.

Keeping at it defines her activism.

"I see it as necessary," she says. "It seems to me that the only way we make change is that people work on it consistently, on a daily basis and in a committed way."

Larry Gabriel is a Detroit-based writer whose work appears in *Metro Times*, where he was formerly the editor. He is a former writer and editor for the *Detroit Free Press* and former editor for the UAW's magazine *Solidarity*.

SNCC Statement on Vietnam War

SNCC's statement against the Vietnam War, published Jan. 6, 1966, was the first by any major civil rights organization. Gloria drafted the statement during a SNCC staff meeting where the issue had been debated at length.

Below is an excerpt from Gloria's handwritten notes. The final text is shown at right.

The SNCC assumes its constitutional right to dissent against the U.S. foreign policy on
and states its opposition to U.S. ~~perpetration~~ involvement in the war in Viet-Nam
on these ~~several~~ grounds:

(1) We ~~do not~~ believe that the Viet Cong are fighting a ... U.S. must ...
~~liberation~~ self-determination. We believe that the ~~Vietnamese~~ ...
not to destroy the Vietnamese people's attempt to establish their
nation and determine the structure of their government ...

~~We believe that the violence perpetrated against black people in the U.S. who are struggling for their freedom is not separate from that~~

(2) We believe the U.S. ~~has been deceptive~~ lies when it claims
concern for the freedom of the Vietnamese people
as it has lied in its claims of concern
for the freedom of other black people both in the U.S. and
~~point out ... could point to many illustrations~~ [illegible]

~~The SNCC advocates immediate withdrawal of U.S. troops from Viet-Nam~~

We understand and support the men in the ... who are
unwilling to ~~enter~~ military service ... and respond

The Student Nonviolent Coordinating Committee has a right and a responsibility to dissent with United States foreign policy on any issue when it sees fit. The Student Nonviolent Coordinating Committee now states its opposition to the United States' involvement in Vietnam on these grounds:

We believe the United States government has been deceptive in its claims of concern for the freedom of the Vietnamese people, just as the government has been deceptive in claiming concern for the freedom of colored people in other countries as the Dominican Republic, the Congo, South Africa, Rhodesia, and in the United States itself.

We, the Student Nonviolent Coordinating Committee, have been involved in the black peoples' struggle for liberation and self-determination in this country for the past five years. Our work, particularly in the South, has taught us that the United States government has never guaranteed the freedom of oppressed citizens, and is not yet truly determined to end the rule of terror and oppression within its own borders.

We ourselves have often been victims of violence and confinement executed by United States governmental officials. We recall the numerous persons who have been murdered in the South because of their efforts to secure their civil and human rights, and whose murderers have been allowed to escape penalty for their crimes.

The murder of Samuel Young* in Tuskegee, Alabama, is no different than the murder of peasants in Vietnam, for both Young and the Vietnamese sought, and are seeking, to secure the rights guaranteed them by law. In each case, the United States government bears a great part of the responsibility for these deaths.

Samuel Young was murdered because United States law is not being enforced. Vietnamese are murdered because the United States is pursuing an aggressive policy in violation of international law. The United States is no respecter of persons or law when such persons or laws run counter to its needs or desires.

We recall the indifference, suspicion and outright hostility with which our reports of violence have been met in the past by government officials.

We know that for the most part, elections in this country, in the North as well as the South, are not free. We have seen that the 1965 Voting Rights Act and the 1964 Civil Rights Act have not yet been implemented with full federal power and sincerity.

We question, then, the ability and even the desire of the United States government to guarantee free elections abroad. We maintain that our country's cry of "preserve freedom in the world" is a hypocritical mask, behind which it squashes liberation movements which are not bound, and refuse to be bound, by the expediencies of United States cold war policies.

We are in sympathy with, and support, the men in this country who are unwilling to respond to a military draft which would compel them to contribute their lives to United States aggression in Vietnam in the name of the "freedom" we find so false in this country.

We recoil with horror at the inconsistency of a supposedly "free" society where responsibility to freedom is equated with the responsibility to lend oneself to military aggression. We take note of the fact that 16% of the draftees from this country are Negroes called on to stifle the liberation of Vietnam, to preserve a "democracy" which does not exist for them at home.

We ask, where is the draft for the freedom fight in the United States?

We therefore encourage those Americans who prefer to use their energy in building democratic forms within this country. We believe that work in the civil rights movement and with other human relations organizations is a valid alternative to the draft. We urge all Americans to seek this alternative, knowing full well that it may cost them their lives – as painfully as in Vietnam.

*Samuel Younge Jr.'s name was misspelled in the original statement.

griot rising

The Volunteer Who Would Become Legacy Keeper

LESLIE REESE

With olive green paneling,

paisley floor tiles and a bar with cushioned elbow rests, Dad had converted the larger part of our basement into a space for the type of grown-folks entertainment that included sipping beers and Harvey Wall-bangers while listening to LP recordings of Redd Foxx, Nipsey Russell, Moms Mabley and Richard Pryor. During the week, it was our family room and the only place in the house that had a television. In 1977, the whole family eagerly descended the basement stairs after dinner for several nights to watch the miniseries *Roots*. It's how we first became acquainted with the term *griot*. We learned that Alex Haley had succeeded in being reconnected to his West African roots, in part because of the griot – a human archive and memorizer-in-chief of history. After *Roots*, many Black American poets, musicians and artists adopted griot to place themselves in the lineage of these African culture-bearers.

That same year, less than three miles from our home in Detroit, the activist-poet Gloria House is asked by the Alexander Crummell Center for Worship and Learning to take up the torch that legendary founder Dudley Randall has had to put down. For he has exhausted himself creating and growing Broadside Press since 1965 from his home. In a decade's time – while still working full-time as a librarian – he catapulted hundreds of unknown Black voices – including such major figures as Sonia Sanchez, Haki Madhubuti, Audre Lorde and Etheridge Knight – onto the literary landscape.

LEFT: Gloria outside the Lafayette Boulevard location of the Broadside Press office, following a Sunday afternoon Broadside Press poetry and theater workshop.

RIGHT: Dudley Randall (in front) at a Broadside Press event at the downtown Detroit library, circa 1989. Behind him, from left to right, are Gloria, Faruq Z. Bey, Murray Jackson and Leslie Reese.

He has worn virtually all the hats, with some assistance from volunteers. Gloria – a volunteer also known by her chosen name, Aneb Kgositsile – is expected to fulfill orders; sell the books, broadsides and other materials; write correspondence; and pay off debts. On her own, she coordinates a collective of volunteers to move Broadside's inventory from Randall's home to the center's basement, the first of several acts of preservation.

She doesn't know it yet, but over the next 50-plus years – revering Randall's monumental cultural contribution to Black people and to the literary world at large – she is going to become the person who stays with the press long after Randall's death in 2000 at age 80.

Already a freedom fighter, cultural worker, educator, wife, mother, and poet, she will sustain and reiterate Broadside's mission, message and spirit, bridging generations and intentions every time the press changes hands. She won't be paid. Gloria will become the connective tissue of this distinct Detroit literary legacy.

She is unaware that she is on her way to becoming a griot.

Gloria House is one of those poets who please not only by their art, but by the revelation of the person behind the art. Ms. House wins the liking of the reader by coming through as a sensitive, vulnerable, gallant woman who feels frustration, loneliness and pain but who does not take the way of alcohol, drugs, or suicide, but affirms:

Yesterday, today and tomorrow
we go on choosing life.

——DUDLEY RANDALL
The late poet and founder of Broadside Press (as written in the foreword to *blood river*, May 1983)

Roles of the West African griot – also known as *jeli* – include "being a political advisor, cultural and social anthropologist, historian, genealogist, mediator, officiator of rites of passage ceremonies, musician, poet and teacher." Not only at Broadside Press, but in her own life and writing as well, Gloria will work as the "quiet warrior" to remember, carry and transport Randall's vision. She will craft her own body of praise songs and poems of love and witness to transmit the memories, gifts and struggles of the community, nourishing the soil that hugs the roots of the people's will.

While a student at Cass Technical High School in 1977, I spend many class hours writing yearning poems and love letters in round, juicy-apple script. It is in interpretive reading class that our instructor, Joseph Taormina, makes suggestions pointing us in the direction of materials we might want to choose from: Tennessee Williams, Edward Albee, the poetry of the Black Arts Movement. "There's always Broadside Press," he says "They publish poetry right here in Detroit."

Gloria opens a reading at Source Books for Steven Ward's book about Grace Lee Boggs, *In Love and Struggle.*
PHOTO: WILLIE WILLIAMS

TOP: Gloria performing at Wayne State University Undergraduate Library at a reading titled Seasons of Struggle, 2007.

BOTTOM: A group of Broadside Press writers gathered just outside the Lafayette Boulevard location of Detroit's Broadside Press in 2005. From left to right: Joan Gartland, Wardell Montgomery, Leslie Reese, Rod Reinhart, Al Ward, Liberty Daniels, M.L. Liebler, Murray Jackson, Regina Reid and her child, Aurora Harris, Gloria House, and poet We Clear The Land.

PHOTO: WILLIE WILLIAMS

With that permission granted, some of us hurried downtown to Vaughn's Bookstore where we knew we could find Black books aplenty. We bypassed the proud, decorous verses that our elder poets had crafted in the European tradition, and went straight for the ones who were turning Black consciousness into poetic forms that were seasoned and informed by our talk and experience, our history and our music. We reached for Black revolutionary love letters, and poems that smelled like the aftermath of burning cities, deep-fried rage, pot liquor and prison.

At Vaughn's we discovered Aneb's poems in *Negro Digest*, or *Black Arts: An Anthology of Black Creations* edited by Ahmed Alhamisi and Harun Kofi Wangara. Published in 1969, inside were poems by Aneb, Randall, Ed Bullins, Carolyn Rodgers, Nikki Giovanni, Larry Neal and others.

Gloria cannot anticipate that, come 1980, Randall, feeling restored, will again take the reins of Broadside Press. Editing and publishing new volumes, and starting up the Broadside Poets Theater at the Crummell Center, he also manages to persuade her to share more of her poems with him.

Taking her "greasy old" manila folder home, Randall proceeds to not only read the poems, but to select and organize a group of them into the manuscript that becomes her first collection, *blood river* (1983).

Gloria and Leslie Reese perform during a memorial tribute for poet Ron Allen during the 2010 African World Festival at Hart Plaza in downtown Detroit.

Aneb doesn't yet know that she is going to author three more poetry collections, has no hint of who she will eventually become to the people, to the city, for dreaming poets like me.

I found my way to Broadside Poets Theater for the first time shortly after dropping out of Spelman College, and just as Aneb's first book was being born. I wanted to make it official that I was going to be a poet. That meant packing my journal and loose sheets of hand-written poems into a messenger bag, donning my crocheted skull cap, and hanging where the Detroit poets were hanging out. I was going with aspirations to join my generation of wordsmiths. I could not have articulated that I wanted to make a connection with my literary path-cutters and the culture, to my city's heritage as a hub of the Black Arts Movement.

It is where I will meet Gloria Aneb: brown and graceful with twinkling eyes. She calls me "little sister." I perceive her modesty and art without espying her conviction, her role as sentinel, as griot.

She makes room for me.

Leslie Reese is a writer, poet and teaching artist. She is the founder of folklore & literacy, which uses books, visual art, music, movement and performance as gateways to literacy and self-expression. Leslie divides her time between Chicago and Detroit.

Broadside Press | Timeline

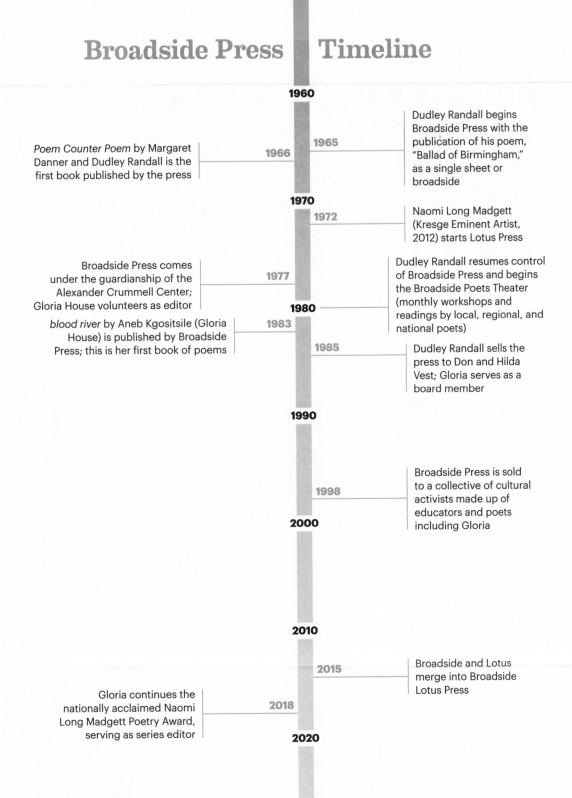

1960

1965 — Dudley Randall begins Broadside Press with the publication of his poem, "Ballad of Birmingham," as a single sheet or broadside

Poem Counter Poem by Margaret Danner and Dudley Randall is the first book published by the press — 1966

1970

1972 — Naomi Long Madgett (Kresge Eminent Artist, 2012) starts Lotus Press

Broadside Press comes under the guardianship of the Alexander Crummell Center; Gloria House volunteers as editor — 1977

Dudley Randall resumes control of Broadside Press and begins the Broadside Poets Theater (monthly workshops and readings by local, regional, and national poets) — 1980

blood river by Aneb Kgositsile (Gloria House) is published by Broadside Press; this is her first book of poems — 1983

1985 — Dudley Randall sells the press to Don and Hilda Vest; Gloria serves as a board member

1990

1998 — Broadside Press is sold to a collective of cultural activists made up of educators and poets including Gloria

2000

2010

2015 — Broadside and Lotus merge into Broadside Lotus Press

Gloria continues the nationally acclaimed Naomi Long Madgett Poetry Award, serving as series editor — 2018

2020

mother to the movement

Gloria House Inspires Across Generations

ILL WEAVER/INVINCIBLE

When I first met Mama Aneb, it was in the early 2000s through Detroit philosopher, writer and activist Grace Lee Boggs. Grace treated young people with respect, asked challenging philosophical questions, and sincerely wondered what solutions younger people had to offer to our world's most pressing crises. The same love and spirit lives in Mama Aneb. In 2010, Mama Aneb and I shared a stage at the United States Social Forum in Detroit where she presented "Ten Lessons from 50 Years of Activism" in honor of Grace's 95th birthday. In it she wrote:

"Protect and secure the children – through alternative educational processes designed to free their minds and prepare them to be creators of a new world; through determined actions against police brutality, war and militarization of our cities; through working for food security and decent housing."

True to this lesson, Mama Aneb spends every Saturday morning with the Detroit Independent Freedom Schools Movement alongside organizers, educators, children and their families. She co-founded the Freedom School project, which exists in the lineage of the Student Nonviolent Coordinating Committee (SNCC) program for which she was once a field secretary in Alabama. During her SNCC days, Mama Aneb and other young organizers were influenced by Ella Baker, who led through deep listening, asking questions, trusting and respecting the people with whom she organized, regardless of their age,

Gloria shares a poem during a reading at the Detroit Historical Society in Detroit, 1998.

experience, or educational background. She could bring forth each individual's unique talents and insights.

Like Baker and Boggs, Mama Aneb embodies facilitative leadership in every interaction she has with young artists and activists, and nurtures intergenerational opportunities for collaboration and conversation.

People hunger for her wisdom. "What kept you going this long in the movement, especially in the face of the double jeopardy of anti-Blackness and patriarchy?" a young black woman asked Mama Aneb during a conversation she was leading in early 2019 at the Charles H. Wright Museum of African American History with Kenyan author and former political prisoner Ngũgĩ wa Thiong'o.

> ## As an emerging curator, arts writer, and publisher of arts criticism from Black perspectives, I have benefited and continue to learn so much from Dr. House and the indelible contributions she's made to Black radical writing platforms.
>
> —— **TAYLOR RENEE ALDRIDGE**
> Writer, independent curator and co-founder of the journal Arts.Black

The woman continued: "And how do you navigate when people in your own community break your heart or betray you?"

With a wrinkle in her brow, Mama Aneb contemplated the question. Then, in a calm, yet powerful voice, she offered: "When people in our community break our heart, it is vital to remember that they are not our enemy, but that their minds are occupied by the same oppressive forces that we are working to liberate ourselves from."

She then offered two main practices that keep her going:

1. Drawing upon the wisdom and strength of our ancestors. Remembering the ways that they survived this, and much worse, so that we could be here, learning and telling their stories.
2. Cultivating community and relationships, especially with those who keep us rooted in integrity, purpose and love, those to whom we return when we need a reprieve from being entrenched in the struggle.

Mama Aneb shares her life and her knowledge with a crystal clarity only made possible through more than 50 years of freedom work: witnessing murder and premature deaths of comrades and loved ones, surviving organizational splits and surveillance, overcoming

TOP: Gloria speaks about the civil rights movement in 2012 at Chippewa Valley High School in Clinton Township, Michigan, at the invitation of a former student who now teaches at the school.

BOTTOM: Gloria at a rally against police brutality with other members of the Detroit Coalition Against Police Brutality, including Detroit activist Ron Scott at the podium, and the group's co-founder, Marge Parsons, in a black T-shirt.

Mama Aneb is a workaholic from the heart. If she tried to sit down and be still, I don't think her bloodline would let her for long. And if you try to give her kudos for all that she does, she'll tell you, "I don't have time for that; I have work to do." There is no stop in her.

—— **ANDREA HETHERU HOUSE**
Detroit teacher, dancer, daughter-in-law

institutional racism in academia justified by bureaucracy, and sharing a lifetime of love and struggle.

Beyond the lessons she provides from decades of work, she values opportunities to listen and be inspired by new approaches to organizing and revolutionary art.

When my arts collective Complex Movements began a multiyear, multimedia exploration of her book *Tower and Dungeon: A Study of Place and Power in American Culture*, we invited Mama Aneb to our studio on the east side of Detroit. We are working with her to redesign and republish the out-of-print book. Although it was released in the early 1990s, *Tower and Dungeon* is more relevant than ever, and at times it reads as a prophetic text. It juxtaposes the Renaissance Center, the 73-story hotel-office complex erected on Detroit's riverfront in the 1970s as a purported symbol of Detroit's rebirth, with what was then known as Jackson State Prison, about 80 miles from Detroit, and once considered the world's largest walled prison, with 5,700 cells:

> The beauty of the RenCen and the ugliness of Jackson State Prison
> do not represent two separate worlds. The same ideology fosters waste
> and opulence on the one hand, and containment, repression, and
> imprisonment on the other. These poles of socio-political reality are

Gloria on a visit to the Western Wall in Jerusalem.

two faces of the same cultural commitment, deeply inscribed in the American landscape. At one end, we have towers of wealth protected by police forces; on the other, we have overcrowded dungeons for dispensable populations. Tower and dungeon – two armed camps serving the same interests, built on the basis of violent dispossession of the people, and maintained by threat of further violence.

Mama Aneb's words offer a visionary model at a moment in Detroit when new skyscrapers and a new jail complex are being built by corporate empires we see stealing public tax subsidies that could otherwise be spent on creating real safety, justice and equitable development in our city.

What a gift it is that she is still organizing for justice, creating new writing and art, shoulder-to-shoulder with us. She understands that time is a continuum, and as long as oppressive forces are dominating the city, we have much work to do. She knows we have much to lose if our stories are not passed across generations, so she cultivates community and relationships, makes time to sit with us and answer questions, listens intently to our visions, affirms that we will make a way out of no way, and reminds us of the many ancestors upon whose legacies we build.

ill Weaver/Invincible is a Detroit-based artist and organizer. They are a member of Complex Movements, an artist and organizing collective supporting the transformation of communities by exploring the connections of complex science and social justice movements through multimedia interactive performance and installation work.

in

praise

and

protest

The Poetry
of Gloria House

Mission

To transcend the wastelands of this lost civilization,
     this murderous world of tasers, smart bombs,
     full metal vests and drones.
To engender on earth
     the new world beauty already alive
     in our heads and hearts.

Incantation

Will words make the way
bearable?
Will they build the ark,
carry us through this flood to Dawn?

Will they soar, lift us out
of this red sea?

Will words, in short,
keep us alive?
Let us call them once more.
Take pen,
faith,
despair,
love,
and pray again.

Meridian, Miss., August, 1964

Disintegrating bodies in black plastic bags
disdain the plump fingers,
    the sags of over-fed stomachs,
    prudent police in burnished holsters
doing their unpleasant duty,
sheepishly,
beneath the American flag.

Fourteen or fifteen years ago,
Chaney, Schwerner and Goodman
Sat tennis-shoed and tee shirted,
    learning how Our Forefathers founded this land
    for freedom's sake.
And they believed.

Have left us now bereaved
and impotent.
Weeping over our Donne and Herbert and T.S. Eliot
Weeping into microphones of mass media.
Weeping at the sight of Goldwater's golden tan.
Weeping
Weeping

Gloria (third from left)
at the Conference
on Black Literature
at Highland Park
Community College
in the 1980s.

Black Women's Affirmation

Can you destroy
the cycle of day and night,
the seasonal flight of birds south?

Yesterday, today and tomorrow,
we go on choosing life.
What do you propose?

Selma, 1965

Amid the ghosts of civil rights marchers
in Selma
in the summer so hot,
the children sang in the paths
of the afternoon showers,
"Before I'd be a slave,
I'd be buried in my grave ..."
From the freedom school window,
we watched them come
across the lawns of the housing project,
down the rain-rutted, dirt roads,
through the puddles waiting cool for bare feet.
(Touch the dripping bush, break a leaf and smell the
pungency of green.)
They were tattered angels of hope,
plaits caught at odd angles
and standing indignantly,
a ripped hem hanging like a train,
grey knees poking through denim frames.
Dancing the whole trip,
they performed their historic drama
against the set of their
wet brick project homes.

Civil Disobedience in My Blood

A Rap against Fascism

The authorities are fascist,
say we're never gonna win.
They've closed off all the exits,
and they're digging graves again.
Never mind, I know I gotta be true to my kin:
Malcolm, Lumumba, Fannie Lou, too.
They're watchin' from afar,
so what can I do?
When you come from this line of furious folk,
you really cannot change it,
ain't about to rearrange it—
hey, I'm happy to proclaim:
I got civil disobedience in my blood,
I got civil disobedience in my blood,
I got civil disobedience in my blood,
I got civil disobedience in my blood.

(Repeat and improvise.)

Seed of the People's New Life

When she has come of age,
she knows it.
The earth feels solid beneath her feet
and there's brown joy in walking,
a rhumba of undulating hips and strong legs.
Moving to ancestral beat,
she be walkin' in rhythm
with the people's music—
they all be singin' their hearts out
and she be travellin' right 'long with 'em.

When she has come of age,
all reality is penetrable,
all doors open,
and death just another door
at the end.

Only life to live.
Only a people to create.
When she has come of age,
she carries in her the seed
of the people's new life.

Each Generation Must Discover Its Mission

(For Frantz Fanon)

Can't you see the distance is long
and the search prolonged anguish?
It may be you will not see the Dawn
and the first sunlight of Day.
What do you say to this possibility?
Can you say, "Yes, that is possible!"
And struggle on in the dark?
Can you accept the questions unanswered,
your mouth frozen as you shape the words?
Perhaps you, in this time, have no words to utter,
only the deep groan of longing
pouring out of the heart,
flowing like a blood river.

For Uri At 16

Though your stretching toward manhood
    has not been without pain—
    father gone, mother tired—
you have risen, a golden presence
    in our midst.

You know the Good,
recognize the Madness,
and move through them both,
floating on your broad smile,
confidence stored in your strong back.

Your eyes flash insight into a world
    we will not know.
You engage the difficult as readily as the easy,
    not baffled by mechanical complexity or
    friends' confusion.
We have watched you recover from intermittent
    fumbles with an athlete's courage;
    observed you dance with fervor,
    caught the first glimpses of your youthful
    wisdom.

Fourth generation son Africa,
You give life to many ancestral shades.
They swing happily forward
    on the energy of your long stride.

Whether it's teaching in the classroom, her poetry, or just showing up at community meetings with her voice, my mom has been trying to touch the world since she got here. I've watched her my whole life, for more than 50 years. Her activism, her art, it's all one.

— URI HERU HOUSE
Gloria's son

Fourth Decade

fully into my fourth decade,
i have wrapped myself in my people's essence,
learned to wear Africa's stole
of dark, soft energy like night vapors
      rising from rainsoaked furrows;

have understood Africa's ancient elegance,
learned to delight in this vibrating
      force field of ancestors about me,
      my invisible escorts,
to relish their discreet company
and hold close my circle of heritage
as some women cling to costly fur.

i feel fine—as my grandmother used to say,
big legs strutting to church in deaconess white
      on Tampa Sundays—
yes, suh, i feel just fine,
fully into my fourth decade.

Sixty

Sixty is far sweeter
than sixteen!
You have survived
a near-century of silly
to arrive at serene—
a lean plateau,
removed from nuisance and nonsense,
from which you view
a new
landscape, through which
you will not careen,
but move in measured steps
to seventy and whatever
lies beyond.

What Is Left?

The seventies are curious years.
They confuse and challenge.
We have lived the long arc of life, but
we are still alive.

If we turn to face life's end,
we may be consumed in that irresistible light.
So we proceed
by backing up,
as a devotee backs from an altar,
towards death,
one step at a time,
while tending to
what is left.

What is left?
To perceive love's revelations.
To pray for the children.
To touch the sick, the lost, the lonely.
To hear the wind's words.
To be rocked by the river's rhythms,
Though we are far from shore.
To greet sleep in joyful abandon to each day's exhaustion.
To rise with questions and await their answers.

That Ray of Sunlight

Seek your sanity
in little things—
clearing lint from the carpet,
celebrating that tidy stack of books and newspapers,
dishes washed and waiting to be put away.

Elude madness
staring at that triangle of river
you drink every morning from the balcony.

Dress your wounds
With cello salve
and gauze of gardenia breezes.

Secure your sanity in that ray of sunlight
heating the window pane.

Gloria with writer
Mari Evans.

Warning to Writers

Writing your soul
will sear streaks
on the white bond,
and the hot glare
emanating from the page
may blind you.

Writing your soul
will sentence you to such silence
you will be thankful
for the soft splatter of rain on the roof,
the creaking of the old house
in the darkness, the city's hum just
before daylight.

Yes, writing your soul
will leave its scar,
render you
the incarnate question mark
that startles and stings.

Gloria accepting the
2019 Kresge Eminent
Artist Award.
PHOTO: PATRICK BARBER

No Justice, No Peace

Martin Luther King Day Rally
Central United Methodist Church
Detroit
January 16, 2012

As long as there are homeless women
      huddled against steaming grates in winter streets;

Long as there are babies whose bodies are lifeless
      from hunger;

Long as our children sit vacant-eyed and sullen
      in what used to be schools;

As long as hundred of thousands of our youth spend
      their most vital years behind bars
      because the rules of the country of their birth
      have contrived it so;

As long as our homes go up in accidental fires in winter
      because corporations have privatized the Earth's energy;

So long as we die of chronic illnesses and much too soon
      because health care is preserved for the rich;

As long as we are turned out of work so that workers abroad
      may be forced into slavery for pennies;

As long as corporate lies grow more preposterous
        as their profits explode;

So long as all these outrages persist,
        we will occupy the streets.

We will occupy the only territory left to us:
        The ground of human dignity,
        The terrain of truth-telling,
        The battle field of "no justice, no peace,"
        No justice, no peace!
        No justice, no peace!

Gloria on the set of
An American Mosaic,
a television program
she co-designed
about cultures
which had been
misrepresented in
traditional history
courses.

In this image she and
her colleague David
Jacobs (at left) are
interviewing Vine
Deloria Jr. (at right),
a Native American
writer and historian.

We Will Stand

Ruthlessly removed from the lands of their birth,
Brought here against their will,
our ancestors chose to survive—
though the days they endured were deadly.
Through centuries of degradation,
they kept choosing to root themselves in the soil of a legacy
that could not be wrenched from them,
a memory of how to stand
in the earth of humanity, to hold their footing
in the ground of Love that sustains everything.

They lifted their voices with tenacity and determination:
We shall not
We shall not
We shall not be moved!
We shall not
We shall not be moved!
Like a tree planted by the water
We shall not be moved!

We have chanted those words in our spirits over generations,
longing for freedom,
for a place where we could feel the earth's throbbing beneath our feet,
and release the bone-deep trepidations
buried in us by centuries of terror.
We sang against lynchings by Klansmen,
Southern sheriffs and other "guardians" of society.
Moving North, we believed, ballot in hand,
we could join the ranks of the free.
We sang.

Those words resounded fifty years ago,
against hosings and dogs and billy clubs,
with our blood running in the streets and the jails.
In the aftermath of assassinations and other horrors,
we retreated into the solace and consolation of those words,
and found the courage to move on.

Now, here in our city, Detroit,
distinguished by its reliable, ingenious workers,
its brilliant political theorists, organizers and visionaries
who have led the nation;
by its geniuses in music and other arts,
who have inspired the world,
by the people's pride in home and neighborhood,
here they intend to dispossess us of the city we know and love.

They have carved out the heart of it for their own pleasure,
and left the rest to wasteland.
By any devious ploy, they intend to take the river and the lakes—
all the water.
They will take the cultural treasures;
they will appropriate the artists,
lure them from the path of truth;
they have bought the politicians and the preachers;
they will write the lies and hand them to the news editors to print;
they have taken our schools and devastated our children;
they intend to silence the righteous.
In a strategic, corporate terrorism,
they intend to leave us hanging in air,
uprooted, displaced.

Who recognizes evil in khaki slacks, navy sports coat and tie?
Who can grasp quickly that those appearing so familiar
mean to scatter us to the wind—
without work, without food, without homes?
Who can take that in?
Hard to fathom though this new treachery may be,
we must be clear-eyed and resolute.

We must sing our song again
and summon the will to stand
like those proud 19th Century African men and women in Detroit,
who, in the face of relentless intimidation,
built churches and schools and mutual aid societies,
and harbored those running to Canada for freedom;
like the sweet doctor, Ossian, who said I will defend my home
from organized violence;
like our grandfathers and fathers, who fought for dignity in the plants,
and the right to unionize to protect the value of their labor;
like all the freedom fighters who made the way for us in this city,
we must stand.

We must keep on choosing to root ourselves in the soil of that legacy
that cannot be ripped out of us, a memory
of how to stand in the earth of our humanity,
to hold our footing in the ground of Love that sustains everything,
and stand like a tree planted by the water,
like Detroiters of old,
like the people of a city planted by the water.
We shall not be moved.
We will stand.
We will stand.
We will stand.

untitled

a poem by **SONIA SANCHEZ,** *for Gloria House*
July 2017

Picture a woman
walking on freedom legs
a sea spray of life ...

Picture her writing
with seditious eyes
loud with life prints ...

Picture her
painting rainbows on a
summer-bent people ...

Picture her rotating
the earth with new words
calling people to be ...

Picture a Sister
Gloria woman tattooing us
with rainbow flesh ...

Picture us listening
To her words ... calling all people
towards new lives becoming ...

Picture a prayer
this woman poet
blessing our eyes.

MONICA MORGAN

87

Gloria with her
granddaughter Isis
(left), her son Uri and
her daughter-in-law
Andrea.

biography

Gloria House

BORN: February 14, 1941
Tampa, Florida

Education

B.A. in French (Minor in
Political Science)
University of California, Berkeley, 1961

Cours Pédagogique Alliance
Française, Paris, 1962

General Secondary
Teaching Credential
University of California, Berkeley, 1964

M.A. in Comparative Literature
University of California, Berkeley,
1969

Ph.D. in American Culture/History
University of Michigan, Ann Arbor,
1986

Professional Appointments

Naomi Long Madgett Poetry Award
Series Editor

Co-Editor, *Riverwise Magazine*, 2016–
present

Professor Emerita, University of
Michigan–Dearborn, 2014

Director of African American Studies,
University of Michigan–Dearborn,
2011–2014

Professor, Humanities and African
American Studies, University of
Michigan–Dearborn, Tenure, 2008

Director of African and African
American Studies, University of
Michigan–Dearborn, 2006–2009

Associate Professor, Humanities and
African American Studies, University
of Michigan–Dearborn, 2003–2008

Writer-in-Residence and Editorial Board Member, Dudley Randall Center for Print Culture, University of Detroit Mercy, 2001–present

Staff Development/Curriculum Specialist and Principal, Timbuktu Academy of Science and Technology, 1999–2003

Arts and Culture Editor, *The Michigan Citizen*, 1998–1999

Associate Professor Emerita, Interdisciplinary Studies, College of Lifelong Learning, Wayne State University, 1998

Director of the Partnership with Township High Schools, and Visiting English Professor University of Witwatersrand, Johannesburg, SA, 1992–1995

Poetry Editor and Contributing Writer, *The Witness*, National Journal of the Episcopal Church Publishing Company, 1991–1999

Associate Professor of Humanities, Interdisciplinary Studies, College of Lifelong Learning, Wayne State University, 1986–98

Assistant Professor of Humanities, Interdisciplinary Studies, College of Lifelong Learning, Wayne State University, 1974–86 (Tenured in 1978)

Instructor, Humanities, Afro-American Literature, Third World and Women's Studies, Monteith College, Wayne State University, 1971–1974

Instructor, Afro-American Literature, English Department, Wayne State University, 1969

Copy Editor, *Detroit Free Press*, 1969–1971

Teacher, French, English, Cass Technical High School, Detroit, Michigan 1967–1968

Field Secretary, Student Non-Violent Coordinating Committee, Lowndes County, Alabama, 1965–1967

Instructor in French, San Francisco State College, Spring, 1965

Teaching Assistant in French and Speech, University of California, Berkeley, 1964–1965

Selected Awards & Honors

Lifetime Achievement Civil Rights Activist Award, Michigan Coalition for Human Rights, 2017

The Edward Said Scholar Activist Award of the Michigan Peace Team, 2012

The Harriet Tubman Award of the National Organization for Women, Wayne County Chapter, 2011

Notable Books of Michigan Award for *A Different Image: The Legacy of Broadside Press. An Anthology*, 2005

The Lillian Benbow Award of Delta Sigma Theta Sorority for Distinguished Service in Education, 1999

President's Award for Excellence in Teaching, Wayne State University, 1991

Poetry Collections

Medicine: New and Selected Poems, University of Detroit Mercy Press and Broadside Lotus Press, 2017

Shrines, Chicago: Third World Press, 2003

Rainrituals, Detroit: Broadside Press, 1989

blood river: poems 1964–1983, Detroit: Broadside Press, 1983

Selected Essays & Other Publications

"Detroit's '67 Rebellion: The Fifty-Year Aftermath," *Annual African American Booklist*, Detroit Main Library, 2017

"The Broadside Press Legacy of Dudley Randall" and "The Undaunted Voices of African American Poets," *Annual African American Booklist*, Detroit Main Library, 2015

Co-author, *Mapping the Water Crisis: The Dismantling of African American Neighborhoods in Detroit*, We the People of Detroit, Research Collective, 2016

"A SNCC Movement Worker Reflects: The Road to Internationalism," *Against the Current*, 2013

Home Sweet Sanctuary: Idlewild Families Celebrate a Century. Detroit: Broadside Press, 2011

"We'll Never Turn Back," *Hands on the Freedom Plow: Personal Accounts by Women in SNCC*. Chicago: University of Illinois Press, September 2010.

A Different Image: The Legacy of Broadside Press. An Anthology. Gloria House (lead editor), Detroit: Broadside Press/University of Detroit Mercy Press, 2004

"Alabama and the Lowndes County Freedom Organization" and "Black Power," commentaries in *A Circle of Trust: Remembering SNCC*, Rutgers University Press, 1998

Tower and Dungeon: A Study of Place and Power in American Culture, Detroit: Casa de Unidad Press, 1991

Selected Affiliations & Community Activism

Board Member, Broadside Lotus Press

Board Member, Volunteer Teacher and Administrator at African-centered schools: Aisha/DuBois Academy, Timbuktu Academy, Nsoroma Academy

Coordinator, Poet-in-Residence Program, a collaborative project of the Detroit Public Library and Broadside Press

Co-Founder, Detroit Coalition Against Police Brutality

Co-Founder, Detroit Justice for Cuba Coalition

Detroit African American Community Council of Elders

Detroit Council of the Arts (Coleman Young administration)

Founding Member, Detroit Independent Freedom Schools Movement

Michigan Coalition for Human Rights

National Council of Elders (of Civil Rights Activists)

We the People of Detroit

bibliography

Gloria House poems reprinted for this publication.

From *Medicine: New and Selected Poems,* Aneb Kgositsile,
Broadside Lotus Press/University of Detroit Mercy Press, 2017.
"Mission"
"Black Women's Affirmations"
"What Is Left?"
"That Ray of Sunlight"
"No Justice, No Peace"
"We Will Stand

From *Shrines,* Aneb Kgositsile, Third World Press, 2004.
"Civil Disobedience in My Blood"
"Sixty"
"Warning to Writers"

From *Rainrituals,* Aneb Kgositsile, Broadside Press, 1989.
"For Uri At 16"
"Fourth Decade"

From *blood river, poems 1964–83,* Aneb Kgositsile, Broadside Press, 1983.
"Incantation"
"Meridian, Miss., August, 1964"
"Selma, 1965"
"Seed of the People's New Life"
"Each Generation Must Discover Its Mission"

our congratulations

The progress thus far of the movement for human rights is a reflection of the visionary and courageous individuals who are gifted with a deep understanding of the path toward liberation, and who risk everything to consistently walk that path in all that they do. Dr. Gloria House is unquestionably one of those individuals.

House's literary work has sparked imagination and action, articulating passionate and compelling ideas, and honoring the impact, sacrifices, joys and humanity of those who have dedicated their lives to the path of freedom. House's activism has registered people to vote, helped lift the voices of the previously unheard, and awakened people to the hypocrisy and futility of war.

We are grateful to the panel of artists and arts professionals who selected House to receive the 2019 Kresge Eminent Artist Award. She not only exemplifies the criteria for the award, but embodies the inspiration and hope of James Weldon Johnson's poem, which stirred her consciousness at a young age:

> Facing the rising sun of our new day begun,
> Let us march on till victory is won.

May we all be as bold in our vision and courageous in our convictions as Dr. Gloria House, and march together until victory is truly won.

CHRISTINA DEROOS
DIRECTOR
KRESGE ARTS IN DETROIT

The Kresge Arts in Detroit program shines a bright light on the extraordinary depth of artistic talent in our midst. Each year, we are reminded of the incredible richness of creativity in this community, and the devotion of Detroit artists to their work. As a poet, activist and educator, Dr. Gloria House's multidimensional career exemplifies the talent, vision and influence that the Kresge Eminent Artist Award exists to recognize.

Dr. House has woven her poetry – including four published collections of work – throughout a life of teaching, mentoring, scholarship and activism. Since retiring from teaching full-time in 2014, her extensive list of contributions and impact have in no way decreased. Instead, through *Riverwise* quarterly magazine, Broadside Lotus Press, We the People of Detroit and the Detroit Independent Freedom Schools Movement, she remains centrally involved in addressing the critical challenges facing Detroit, including the local water shutoff crisis, liberatory education and land use justice.

Dr. House is a soldier for social justice and the epitome of the engaged artist. Her achievements leave no question as to why she was selected to join the small number of exceptional individuals who have thus far received the lifetime achievement honor. Her work is an invaluable literary gift and an indispensable quest for equity, understanding and a more just society. The College for Creative Studies is proud to partner with The Kresge Foundation to celebrate Dr. House's lifelong commitment to creativity and the advancement of human rights.

RICHARD ROGERS
PRESIDENT
COLLEGE FOR CREATIVE STUDIES
(JULY 1994–JUNE 2019)

the kresge eminent artist award and winners

Established in 2008, the Kresge Eminent Artist Award honors an exceptional literary, fine, film or performing artist whose influential body of work, lifelong professional achievements and proven, continued commitment to the Detroit cultural community are evident. The Kresge Eminent Artist Award celebrates artistic innovation and rewards integrity and depth of vision with the financial support of $50,000. The Kresge Eminent Artist Award is unrestricted and is given annually to an artist who has lived and worked in Wayne, Oakland or Macomb counties for a significant number of years.

The Kresge Eminent Artist Award, annual Kresge Artist Fellowships, Gilda Awards, and multiyear grants to arts and cultural organizations in metropolitan Detroit constitute Kresge Arts in Detroit, the foundation's core effort to provide broad support to the regional arts community.

The College for Creative Studies administers the Kresge Eminent Artist Award on behalf of The Kresge Foundation.

NICK SOUSANIS

Charles McGee, 2008

JUSTIN MACONOCHIE

Marcus Belgrave, 2009

PAUL DAVIS

Bill Harris, 2011

LON HORWEDEL

Naomi Long Madgett, 2012

MICHIGAN OPERA THEATRE

David DiChiera, 2013

MICHELLE ANDONIAN

Bill Rauhauser, 2014

ELLY STEWART

Ruth Adler Schnee, 2015

JULIE PINCUS

Leni Sinclair, 2016

JULIE PINCUS

Patricia Terry-Ross, 2017

NOAH ELLIOTT MORRISON

Wendell Harrison, 2018

The 2019 Kresge Eminent Artist Selection Committee

DR. GLORIA HOUSE was named the 2019 recipient of the Kresge Eminent Artist Award by a distinguished group of artists and arts professionals. The panel included for the first time a previous Kresge Eminent Artist, Bill Harris.

JUANITA ANDERSON
Filmmaker, Director of Media Arts and Studies, Wayne State University Department of Communications

BILL HARRIS
Playwright, Poet, Novelist, Emeritus Professor, Wayne State University 2011 Kresge Eminent Artist

NJIA KAI
Special Events and Programming Director, NKSK Events + Production

MARSHA MUSIC
Writer, Poet, Storyteller, 2012 Kresge Artist Fellow

MICHELLE PERRON
Director, Office of Exhibitions & Public Programs, College for Creative Studies; Founding Director, Kresge Arts in Detroit

MARK STRYKER
Detroit Free Press Arts Reporter and Critic (1995–2016); Author, *Jazz from Detroit* (forthcoming, University of Michigan Press), 2012 Kresge Artist Fellow

about the
kresge foundation

THE KRESGE FOUNDATION was founded in 1924 to promote human prog-
ress. Today, Kresge fulfills that mission by building and strengthening pathways
to opportunity for low-income people in America's cities, seeking to dismantle
structural and systemic barriers to equality and justice. Using a full array of
grant, loan and other investment tools, Kresge invests more than $160 million
annually to foster economic and social change.

Board of Trustees

index

This index is sorted letter-by-letter. Italic page locators indicate photographs on the page.

acknowledgements

With immense gratitude to Dr. Gloria House for the time, knowledge, wisdom and generosity of spirit she shared for this publication. As the copyright holder of her poetry and writing, Dr. Gloria House has graciously permitted The Kresge Foundation to reproduce and excerpt her work.

Sincere thanks also go to Larry Gabriel, Leslie Reese and ill Weaver/Invincible for their contributions.

credits

NICHOLE CHRISTIAN
Creative Director, Editor, Writer

PATRICK BARBER
Art Director, Graphic Designer,
Photographer

RIP RAPSON
President and CEO
The Kresge Foundation

JENNIFER KULCZYCKI
Director, External Affairs &
Communications
The Kresge Foundation

JULIE A. BAGLEY
Assistant, External Affairs
& Communications
The Kresge Foundation

W. KIM HERON
Senior Communications Officer
The Kresge Foundation

ALEJANDRO HERRERA
Graphic Designer
The Kresge Foundation

PRINTER
KTD Print, Royal Oak, Michigan

PHOTOGRAPHY

Unless otherwise noted, photos used throughout this monograph are from the personal collection of Dr. Gloria House. Every effort has been made to locate and credit the holders of copyrighted materials.

Photographs of Dr. House on the frontispiece and pages 1, 4 and 98 are by Patrick Barber.

Copies of this monograph and others in the Eminent Artist series are available at no cost (while supplies last) by emailing your name and mailing address to **monographs@kresge.org**

All monographs are also available for download via
https://kresge.org/EAmonographs